THEOLOGY FOR AMATEURS

Also by Alister McGrath

NIV Bible Commentary
The Enigma of the Cross
Evangelicalism and the Future of Christianity
A Journey through Suffering
Roots that Refresh
To Know and Serve God
Understanding Doctrine

Theology for Amateurs

Alister McGrath

Series Editor: Michael Green

Hodder & Stoughton

LONDON   SYDNEY   AUCKLAND

British Library Cataloguing in Publication Data
A record for this book is available from the British Library

ISBN 0 340 74553 3

Typeset by Avon Dataset Ltd, Bidford-on-Avon, Warks

Printed and bound in Great Britain by
Clays Ltd, St Ives plc

Hodder and Stoughton Ltd
A Division of Hodder Headline PLC
338 Euston Road
London NW1 3BH

Contents

From the Editor . . .

This is the second book in a series '*. . . for amateurs*'. We are convinced that many people are interested in looking at basic issues in the Christian faith, but feel they do not know enough to embark on the massive tomes which gather dust on library shelves. So we are putting out a series of books on important aspects of Christianity in a very accessible form, illustrated by the incomparable Taffy Davies, who is both a cartoonist and a clergyman.

The first book in the series was my own *Evangelism for Amateurs*. The prime task of the worshipping community is to spread the good news of Jesus to those who do not yet know him, and we are not very good at that! So that book attempts to address this situation.

Now a very distinguished British theologian, Dr Alister McGrath, helps us to come to grips with the importance of theology. He does so with compelling clarity and a wonderful, attractive simplicity. And that is something you might not expect from a lecturer in the University of Oxford and the principal of a theological college. But one of the great accomplishments of Alister McGrath is his rare ability to produce massive theological tomes for the theologians, and also to write with bewitching lucidity for the likes of you and me! Read on, and you will see what I mean!

Michael Green
Series Editor

1

Why bother with theology?

Most of us find it easy to talk about things that we enjoy. Our enthusiasm can be infectious, causing others to want to share our interests. So what could be more natural for Christians than talking about their faith? Talking about God is as natural as it is important.

Most technical terms are based on the Greek language. Words ending in '-ology' are based on the Greek word *logos*, which means something like 'talk' or 'discussion'. Thus 'biology' means 'talk about life' (from the Greek word *bios*, 'life'). 'Theology' is thus 'talk about God' (from the Greek word *theos*, 'God'). In one sense, we are all theologians, in that we all want to talk about God. Yet it is not quite as simple as that.

Most Christians do not think theology to be important. I write these words with sadness. Yet it is important to be honest about this before we go any further. Theology is widely seen, even by the most enthusiastic Christian believers, as rather pointless speculation undertaken by people who ought to be doing something more useful with their lives – like pastoring churches or working on the mission field.

As someone who believes that theology is enormously exciting – something that brings new depth and wonder to our faith – I find this attitude not a little disheartening. Yet I can understand it. Having taught theology at Oxford University for many years, I am only too aware that lots of theological writings are difficult to read, overloaded with jargon, and seem to have little relevance to the deepening of personal faith or the encouragement of the mission of the Church. But it does not have to be like this.

This book is written in the belief that Christian theology is one of the most wonderful subjects that anyone can hope to study. If you have tried to wrestle with it, and turned away dissatisfied or discouraged, why not give it another chance? This book is going to introduce you to theology on the assumption that you know nothing about it. If you have had a discouraging encounter with it before, forget it. Let's start all over again. And as we explore theology together, we can understand its importance by seeing it in action.

So where shall we begin? Perhaps with one of the simplest, yet most profound, of biblical statements – 'The Lord is my shepherd' (Psalm 23:1).

2

Exploring an image: God as a shepherd

'The Lord is my shepherd' (Psalm 23:1). This is one of the most familiar biblical passages. Many Christians find it immensely comforting and reassuring, especially when going through difficult times. But what does it mean? And how does it help us understand why theology helps us with our faith?

What springs to mind when we talk of a shepherd? In biblical times, the shepherd was someone who was in charge of a flock of sheep. He would lead them as they wandered through the desert, trying to find food and water for them, and protecting them against wild animals. So what is this saying about God?

We need to be clear from the start that thinking about 'God as a shepherd' does *not* mean that God is a human being who spends his time leading lots of four-legged animals about in a desert. All the shepherds that we know are human beings. At first sight, the biblical passage we are examining might therefore seem to imply that God is human. Yet this is clearly not the case, and is certainly

not what the biblical passage means.

The Bible uses *analogies* to speak about God. If I were to say that A is an analogy for B, I am not saying that A is identical with B. I am simply stating that there are points of likeness between them, just as there are points of difference. And we all know that analogies break down if we press them too far! Yet analogies allow us to think of complicated or difficult things by using simple and familiar ideas.

To speak of 'God as a shepherd' is to affirm that 'God is *like* a shepherd'. In other words, the image of a shepherd helps us think about the nature of God, and allows us to gain insights into his nature. It does not mean that God is *identical* to a human shepherd. Rather, it means that some aspects of a human shepherd help us think about God and appreciate him better.

Let's put this into practice by drawing up a list of things that are true about shepherds.

1 Shepherds are human beings.
2 Shepherds look after sheep.
3 Shepherds protect their sheep against danger.
4 Shepherds lead their sheep to food and water.

Now let's look at each of these in turn, and see what we can learn about God from them.

First, all the shepherds that we are familiar with are human beings. It is quite clear that this does not mean that we are to think of God as a human being. This is clearly one aspect of the analogy that we are not meant to pursue. God is *not* a human being; yet the behaviour

of one particular group of human beings is seen as helping us to get a better grasp on the nature of God himself. So let us agree that this is one aspect of the analogy which we are not meant to press too far.

Second, shepherds lead sheep. What does that tell us? Interestingly, this aspect of the analogy helps us to understand something important about ourselves. It invites us to think of ourselves as sheep. Initially, this seems rather strange, and perhaps even a little insulting. After all, sheep are not the most intelligent of animals. They are always getting lost and getting stuck in hedges. Yet the Bible uses the sheep as an image of fallen human nature. Thinking of ourselves as sheep reminds us that we are lost, and need someone to find us and bring us home safely. It may not be a very complimentary way of thinking about ourselves. Yet it is totally realistic!

Recognising our need for a shepherd means both that we need to be saved, and that we cannot save ourselves. Jesus told a parable about a lost sheep (Luke 15) to emphasise this point. Even though ninety-nine sheep were safely in the fold, protected against danger, the shepherd went out in search of one lost sheep. Unaided, the sheep could not make its way home. When the shepherd found it, he carried it home to safety. Maybe the sheep was injured or tired. Maybe it was just lost, and had no idea where it was. Yet the shepherd went to find it, because it mattered to him. God is like that shepherd. He wants to find those who are lost, and bring them home to safety.

Third, shepherds protect their sheep against danger. We can see here a wonderful and very moving statement of the love of God for us, and his determination to look after us. The image of a shepherd guarding his flock against wild animals reminds us that God cares for us, and wants to protect us against all the dangers that lie in wait for us as we travel along the road of faith. The New Testament refers to Jesus as 'the good shepherd' – a shepherd who is prepared to lay down his life for his sheep (John 10). This brings home to us the amazing extent of God's love for us.

Fourth, the shepherd leads the sheep to food and water. On their own, they could not find these vital resources, and would die. The shepherd leads the sheep to them, and guards them while they eat and drink. This powerful analogy reminds us that God provides us with all that we need on the journey of faith. Just as God provided Israel with manna from heaven to sustain her on the long journey from Egypt to the promised land, so he will sustain us as well on our journey to the New Jerusalem.

So do you see how the analogy of God as a shepherd gives added depth to the great themes of the Christian faith? To be sure, we can know about the love of God for his people without needing to think about a shepherd. Yet the image of a shepherd gives added depth and vividness to this theme. It is easy to think of the love of God in very abstract terms. The image of a shepherd brings the idea of the love of God vividly to life. It makes us think of a real-life situation in which love and care can be seen in action.

Now why does the Bible use analogies like this? Well, how else could we begin to understand God? How could we get our minds round him? Some early Christian writers used to compare understanding God with looking directly into the sun. The human eye is simply not capable of withstanding the full brilliance of the sun. In the same way, the human mind cannot cope with the full glory of God.

The story is told of the pagan emperor who visited the Jewish rabbi Joshua ben Hananiah. The emperor asked to be allowed to see Joshua's god. The rabbi replied that this was impossible, an answer which failed to satisfy the emperor. So the rabbi took the emperor outside, and asked him to stare at the midday summer sun. 'Impossible!' replied the emperor. 'If you cannot look at the sun, which God created,' replied the rabbi, 'how much less can you behold the glory of God himself!'

As every amateur astronomer knows, however, it is possible to look at the sun through a piece of dark glass. This greatly reduces the brilliance of the sun, so that the human eye can cope with it. Otherwise, looking at the sun would be completely beyond its capacities. In much the same way, it is helpful to think of the scriptural models or pictures of God as revealing God in manageable proportions, so that the human mind can cope with him.

John Calvin (1509–64), widely regarded as one of the greatest Christian theologians, argued that God knows our limited ability to cope with ideas, and thus reveals himself in ways that we can handle. This does not reflect any weakness or inadequacy on God's part. It is simply a reflection of God's generous and kindly nature, by which he takes our weakness into account when revealing himself. Calvin comments that 'God accommodates himself to our ability' – meaning that God uses words, ideas and images that we can relate to. The Bible is packed full of powerful and vivid images of God, which allow us to appreciate the full wonder and glory of God.

So what does this tell us about theology? One of the great roles of theology is to help us sort out what we mean when we talk about God. Most Christians have given very little thought to the content of their faith. They use words and images lightly, and fail to appreciate their depth and richness. Theology forces us to ask questions like: 'What do you mean when you say that God is our shepherd?' And by forcing us to *think*, it offers us the opportunity to deepen our understanding and appreciation of our faith.

Far too many Christians have little more than a superficial understanding of their faith. Theology issues a challenge to a complacent and superficial faith.

- It declares that there is more to our faith than we know.
- It challenges us to go deeper.
- It offers us the possibility of enriching our faith.

Theology is about serving God with our minds. It is about allowing the love of God we know in our hearts to affect the way in which we think about God. Theology is about taking trouble to make sure that we get God right.

Let's take this a stage further. We have seen the value of theology in exploring an *image* of God. Now we shall look at how we go about making sense of an *event*, focussing especially on the cross of Christ.

3

Exploring an event: the cross of Christ

The Christian faith is grounded in events, above all the weekend that changed the world – the crucifixion and resurrection of Jesus. Christianity offers a vision of history as the arena in which God is working out his great purposes of redemption.

Events need to be interpreted. Their meaning needs to be drawn out. One of the great tasks of theology is to ensure that we extract the full and proper meaning of the great events on which the Christian faith is founded. In this chapter, we shall look at one event in particular – the cross.

The first issue we need to explore is the relation between an event and its meaning. For some, it might at first seem to be enough to declare that Jesus was crucified and he rose again. Why add more? Let's begin by agreeing that it is essential to the Christian faith that these events really took place. The Christian faith would be a hollow sham if Jesus never existed, if there was no cross, and if Jesus never rose from the dead. If those

events did not happen, then the credentials of Christianity are destroyed.

Yet the gospel is more than declaring historical events! The English reformer William Tyndale referred to this way of thinking about the gospel as a 'story-book faith'. Yet there is a lot more to the gospel than simply agreeing that certain things really did happen back in first-century Palestine.

It is not so much the *events* of the crucifixion and resurrection themselves, as their *significance* for believers which lies at the heart of the Christian faith. Let's compare two statements:

1 Jesus died.
2 Jesus died *for the forgiveness of our sins.*

The first of these is an historical statement. It is unquestionably a very important historical statement – but it does nothing more than affirm that something happened. The second also makes an historical statement. But it adds something else – an *interpretation* of the significance of this historical event for us. That difference is vital. Something really happened – but it possesses a deeper meaning. It is essential that this deeper meaning is unfolded.

Paul makes this point when he declares that 'Christ died for our sins' (1 Corinthians 15:3). It is not just the historical fact of the death of Christ that is of such importance; it is what that event means for us. Jesus died to bring us forgiveness. His death affects us, and brings us benefits. The better we understand our faith, the more we will appreciate it! So digging deeper into the bedrock of faith will help us get a better grasp of the gospel, and equip us to tell others about it.

Yet the cross possesses a richness of meaning which is difficult to summarise briefly. It is rather like a great work of architecture, such as a palace or cathedral. To fully appreciate the building, we need to see it from various angles. We need to examine every aspect of its stonework, and admire the intricacy of its design and carving. We shall never appreciate the immense amount of labour that went into its building, or fully grasp its beauty, if we only give it a casual glance. We need to examine the cross from different angles, if we are to do justice to the rich tapestry of biblical reflection on its meaning and relevance.

So what are we to make of the cross? We could think of the cross as being like an artistic masterpiece – perhaps a Flemish landscape. We can stand well back from the painting, and admire the overall view. Or we could focus in on a small part of the painting, admiring the intricacy of the brush-strokes and the highly effective use of colours.

Perhaps the best way of 'standing back' from the cross is to read one of the passion narratives in the gospels, which tell the story of the betrayal, trial, crucifixion and death of Jesus. These powerful and highly evocative accounts of the last days of the human life of Jesus will allow us to gain a sense of the pain which he suffered, and bring home to us the *costliness* of redemption. The Son of God had to suffer and to die so that we might live. That thought is more than enough to bring us to our knees.

Yet we can then move on, and begin to explore the fine detail of the cross. One major theme is that the penalty due for our sin has been paid by Christ on the cross. Our guilt has been purged by his life-giving and cleansing blood. This point is made powerfully by Mrs Cecil F. Alexander in her famous hymn 'There is a Green Hill Far Away':

> There was no other good enough
> To pay the price of sin;
> He only could unlock the gate
> Of heaven, and let us in.

The price paid by God to achieve our forgiveness was high; his Son died in order that we might be forgiven. This amazing thought helps us realise how much God loves us. It might also give us an idea of how much we should love God in return!

But how can the death of Christ have this effect? To explore this point, we shall look at the answer given by a professional theologian – the eleventh-century theologian Anselm of Canterbury. God created humanity in order that we might have eternal life. Unfortunately, sin intervened to make it impossible for us to gain eternal life unaided. If we are to have eternal life, God will have to do something about it.

God cannot just pretend that sin doesn't exist, or dismiss it as unimportant. It is a force which threatens to disrupt all that God intends for his creation. A remedy must be found for sin which undoes its effects yet takes its moral aspects seriously. Anselm stresses that sin is a moral problem. It cannot just be ignored; it must be confronted and dealt with.

So how can the offence of sin be purged? How can sin be forgiven justly, in a way that acknowledges both the offence caused to God by sin and his loving-kindness?

In answering these questions, Anselm draws an analogy from the feudal outlook of the period. In ordinary life, an offence against a person can be forgiven, provided that some sort of compensation is given for the offence. Anselm refers to this compensation as a 'satisfaction'. For example, a man might steal a sum of money from his neighbour. In order to meet the demands of justice, the man would have to restore that sum of money, plus an additional sum for the offence given by the theft in the first place. It is this additional sum of money which is the 'satisfaction' in question.

Anselm argues that sin is a serious offence against God, for which a satisfaction is required. As God is infinite, this satisfaction must also be infinite. But as we are finite, we cannot pay this satisfaction. So it seems impossible that we shall ever have eternal life.

Yet this is not the end of the matter! God wishes us to be saved – yet saved in a way that protects *both* God's mercy and his righteousness. Although we, as sinful human beings, ought to pay the satisfaction due for our sin, the simple fact is that we cannot. We just do not have the resources or the ability to meet this debt.

On the other hand, although God is under no obligation to pay the satisfaction, he clearly could do so if he wanted to. So, Anselm argues, it is quite clear that a God-man would be both able and obliged to pay this satisfaction. Therefore the death of Jesus Christ, as the Son of God, is the means by which this dilemma can be resolved.

As a human being, Christ has an obligation to pay the satisfaction; as God, he has the ability to pay it. The satisfaction is thus paid off, and we are enabled to regain eternal life. Anselm's theory showed how the death of Christ enabled God to forgive our sin without flouting his justice.

This short example of theological analysis shows how theology helps us to make sense of the cross. The connection between the death of Christ on the cross and our redemption is neither *non-existent* nor is it *arbitrary*. As Anselm shows, there is a real and important relationship between the cross and forgiveness. This relation allows us to make sense of the cross, and also to gain an increased awareness of the wonder both of our redemption and of the God who so graciously redeems us.

Having explored how theology makes sense of events, let's move on, and look at the value of theology in clarifying the way we talk about God. What does it mean to say that God is 'almighty'?

4

Exploring an idea: God almighty

We all know how the Creed begins: 'I believe in God, the Father almighty.' Suppose we pause at this point, and ask what we mean when we say that God is 'almighty'?

At first sight, this might seem to be something of a waste of time. 'Almighty' is a perfectly simple word. It means 'capable of doing anything'. And as we believe that God is indeed almighty, we are simply saying that God can do anything. Why bother wasting time on a pointless discussion about such an obvious matter?

One of the tasks of theology is to make us think about what we really mean when we talk about God. And as talking about God is a serious matter, we must ensure that we get him right. Clearly, thinking seriously about such 'obvious' matters is important if we are to be faithful to God. But it also helps us understand more about the distinctive nature and character of the God who we know and love.

Let's begin with a simple statement. 'To say that God is almighty means that God can do anything.' At first,

this seems fairly straightforward. On reflection, it's not that simple. Think about the following question: 'Can God draw a triangle with four sides?' It does not take much thought to see that this question has to be answered with the word 'No'. Triangles have three sides; to draw something with four sides is to draw a quadilateral, not a triangle.

Now try thinking about a more complicated question. 'Can God create a stone which is too heavy for him to lift?' This question involves a nice logical puzzle. If God cannot create such a stone, there is something that he cannot do. Yet if God can create such a stone, then he will not be able to lift it – and so there is something else he cannot do. Whatever way the question is answered, God's ability to do anything is called into question.

However, on reflection, it is not clear that these questions cause problems for the Christian understanding of God. Four-sided triangles do not and cannot exist. The fact that God cannot make such a triangle is not a serious issue. It just forces us to restate our simple statement in a more complicated way. 'To say that God is almighty means that God can do anything that does not involve logical contradiction.'

Yet we need to go deeper than this.

If we explore the nature of God's power, we begin to realise the wonderful and amazing way in which he relates to us. To understand this, we need to look at another question. 'Can God make someone who loves him hate him?' At first sight, the question seems a little strange. Why should God want to turn someone's love for him into a hatred? The question appears unreal and pointless.

On closer examination, however, the question begins to make sense. At one level, there is no problem. 'To say that God is almighty means that God can do anything that does not involve logical contradiction.' Well, there is clearly no contradiction involved here. God must have the ability to turn someone's love into hatred. Yet there is obviously a deeper issue here, concerning the character of God himself. Can we ever imagine God wanting to do this?

To make this important point clearer, let us ask another question. 'Can God break his promises?' There is no logical contradiction involved in breaking promises. It happens all the time. It may be regrettable, but there is no intellectual problem here. If God can do anything that does not involve a logical contradiction, he can certainly break a promise.

Yet, for Christians, this suggestion is outrageous. The God we know and love is one who remains faithful to his promises. If we cannot trust God, whom can we trust? The suggestion that God might break a promise contradicts a vital aspect of God's character – his total faithfulness and truthfulness.

There is a tension between power and trust. An all-powerful cheater can make promises which cannot be relied upon. Yet one of the greatest insights of the Christian faith is that we know a God who *could* do anything – but who *chose* to redeem us. And having committed himself, he remains faithful to his promises. We have the privilege of knowing a God who has chosen to stay with us.

The Old Testament expresses this idea in terms of a

covenant – an agreement by which God binds himself to be our God, and to care for us. Nobody forced God to do that. He didn't have to do it. Yet he chose to do so. Why? Because God loves us. He didn't have to redeem us. But he chose to do this. When we look at the great theme of redemption, we can begin to see how much this tells us about the wonder of our God.

In this chapter, we have seen the importance of making sure we understand what we mean when we use words to talk about God. Talking about 'God almighty' might seem to suggest that God can do anything – like break his promises. As we explored this idea in more detail, a far more satisfying and powerful idea emerged.

God is one who has committed himself to our redemption, because he loves us so much. We can rely on him to achieve his purpose. So the word 'almightiness' – as used by Christians – does not mean 'God's ability to do *anything*' but 'God's ability to achieve his purposes'. God does not do things that are logical contradictions or which deny his character. Instead, he works to achieve his purposes. And what are those purposes? Well, one of them is to save us. Let us rejoice that we are dealing with a God who does not just *promise* us salvation; he has the ability to achieve it. 'The one who calls you is faithful and he will do it' (1 Thessalonians 5:24).

In the next chapter, we shall develop this idea of exploring words still further, as we look at the importance of unpacking the full meaning of key terms in the Christian vocabulary.

5

Jargon-busting: unpacking
Christian words

Theology forces us to explain what we mean when we talk about God. All too often – and sometimes without being aware of it! – Christians fall into the habit of using jargon. They talk about things like 'being saved'. The vocabulary of many Christian sermons will certainly include rich and stimulating terms, such as 'redemption' and 'salvation'. Yet these can easily become words which we use without really understanding.

One of the greatest weaknesses of modern Christianity is its parrot-like repetition of key words and phrases *without* appreciating the spiritual riches which they represent. We need to unpack the meaning of these terms, and make sure that we have understood and appreciated their meaning and relevance. The well-known amateur theologian C. S. Lewis once made this point as follows:[1]

[1]C. S. Lewis, God in the Dock (*Grand Rapids, MI: Eerdmans, 1970), p. 96.*

I have come to the conclusion that if you cannot translate your own thoughts into uneducated language then your thoughts are confused. Power to translate is the test of having really understood your own meaning.

This is where theology comes into its own. Theology is about the unpacking of Christian words. It dissects them, and allows us to see their fine detail. Here are a few examples.

We begin by looking at a New Testament term used to illuminate the meaning of the death of Christ – ransom.

Jesus himself declared that he came 'to give his life as a ransom for many' (Mark 10:45). The idea is also found elsewhere. In 1 Timothy 2:5–6, Paul speaks of Jesus Christ being a 'mediator between God and humanity . . . who gave his life as a ransom for all'. A ransom is a price which is paid to achieve someone's freedom.

In the Old Testament, however, the emphasis falls upon the idea of being freed, of liberation, rather than speculation about the nature of the price paid, or the identity of the person to whom it is paid. Thus Isaiah 35:10 and 51:11 refer to the liberated Israelites as the 'ransomed of the Lord'. The basic idea is that God intervenes to deliver his people from captivity, whether from the power of Babylon (Isaiah 51:10–11) or of death (Hosea 13:14).

To speak of Jesus' death as a 'ransom' suggests three ideas.

First, it hints at the idea of someone being held in bondage. To many readers of the New Testament, it might evoke the image of some great public figure being held captive, against his or her will. Their freedom depends totally upon someone being prepared to pay the ransom demand.

This brings us to the second idea which is prompted by the image of a 'ransom' – that of a price which is paid to bring about the freedom of the captive. The more important the person being held to ransom, the greater the price demanded. One of the most astonishing things about the love of God for us is that he was prepared to pay so dearly to set us free. The price of our freedom was the death of his one and only Son (John 3:16).

And third, it reminds us that the death and resurrection of Jesus are liberating. We are set free! The New Testament reminds us that Jesus has set us free from the fear of death (Hebrews 2:14–15), and brought us into the glorious freedom of the children of God.

All these ideas are present in the word 'ransom'. By taking the trouble to unpack its meaning, we are deepening the quality of our faith. It is like cracking the hard shell of a nut, and uncovering the sweet kernel within. Thinking about words like 'ransom' unlocks the spiritual and intellectual richness of the Christian faith. It reminds us that Christianity saves our souls, warms our hearts and nourishes our minds.

Another word used in the New Testament to refer to the achievement of Christ on the cross is 'adoption'. Paul uses this word to help explain the benefits which result from Christ's death (Romans 8:15; 8:23; 9:4; Galatians 4:5; Ephesians 1:5). So what does he mean? What does he expect his readers to make of this?

Adoption was not something that happened in Judaism. The word actually comes from Roman family law, with which Paul (and many of his readers, particularly at Rome!) would have been familiar. Under this law, a father was free to adopt individuals from outside his natural family, and give them the legal status of being his children. Although there is still a real distinction between natural and adopted children, they have the same legal status. In the eyes of the law, they are all members of the same family, irrespective of their origins.

Paul uses the term 'adoption' to indicate that, through faith, believers come to have the same status as Jesus (as sons of God), without implying that they have the same divine nature as Jesus. Faith brings about a change in our status before God, incorporating us within the family of God, despite the fact that we do not share the same divine origins as Christ. Coming to faith in Christ thus brings about a change in our status. We are adopted into the family of God, with all the benefits that this brings.

What benefits? Two may be singled out. First, to be a member of the family of God is to be an heir of God. Paul argues this point as follows. If we are adopted as children of God, we share the same inheritance rights as the natural child. We are thus 'heirs of God' and 'co-heirs with Christ' (Romans 8:17), for we share in the same inheritance rights as him.

Just as Christ suffered and was glorified, so shall we. All that Christ has inherited from God will one day be ours as well. For Paul, this insight is of considerable importance in understanding why believers undergo

suffering. Christ suffered before he was glorified; believers must expect to do the same. Just as suffering for the sake of the gospel is real, so is the hope of future glory, as we will share in all that Christ has won by his obedience.

Second, adoption into the family of God brings a new sense of belonging. Everyone needs to feel that they belong somewhere. Social psychologists have shown the need for a 'secure base', a community or group which gives people a sense of purpose and an awareness of being valued and loved by others. In human terms, this need is usually met by the family unit. For Christians, this real psychological need is met through being adopted into the family of God. Believers can rest assured that they are valued within this family, and are thus given a sense of self-confidence which enables them to work in and witness to the world.

These two examples show how theology can enhance our evangelism. By making sure that we understand our faith, and its immense spiritual and intellectual richness, we can make our evangelism more effective. To understand our faith we need to unlock its richness. This ensures that we proclaim the Christian faith for all its immense worth. The Christian who has never thought about her faith is likely to be a poor evangelist. Why? Because she has never taken the trouble to understand her faith, she will experience serious difficulty when she tries to explain it to others. Understanding our faith is an essential precondition for good evangelism!

Do you see how we have already established a link between theology and evangelism? We shall follow this through as this book develops, and see how theology can help us become more effective evangelists. Meanwhile, we move on to see how theology links up with the Bible.

6

The foundation: theology and the Bible

Jesus loves me, this I know.
For the Bible tells me so.

It may seem a little strange to open this chapter with a quotation from a children's hymn. Yet so often the most important things in life *can* be said simply! These simple lines point us to the *focus* and *foundation* of theology. The focus is Jesus, and the love which he shows for each and every one of us. And the foundation of all our knowledge of Jesus, and of God, is the Bible. Theology is grounded in Scripture and focussed on Jesus. We shall be looking later at some of the insights about Jesus which are so central to our faith. For the moment, let us think about the vitally important role of the Bible in theology.

Theology is based on the Bible. Christians see the Bible as the source of true and reliable knowledge of God, Jesus and ourselves. It is a secure foundation on which we can build our thinking. So how does theology relate to the Bible?

The main thing to note here is the immense richness of the Bible. It is not easy to do justice to the magnificent vistas that it opens up. The Bible throws open a window which allows us to see something of the nature and purposes of God. Theology attempts to explore and describe what we find in its pages.

A helpful way of thinking of the relation of theology to the Bible was put forward by the great nineteenth-century Scottish preacher Thomas Guthrie. This approach is based on the different environments in which flowers grow. Guthrie argued that the Bible is like nature. Here, flowers and plants grow freely in their natural habitat, unordered by human hands. The human desire for orderliness leads to these same plants being collected and arranged in botanical gardens according to their species, in order that they can be individually studied in more detail. The same plants are found in different contexts – one of which is natural, the other of which is the result of human ordering. Theology represents the human attempt to order the ideas of Scripture, arranging them in an orderly way so that their mutual relation can be better understood.

Seen in this way, theology is not – and was never meant to be – a substitute for Scripture. Rather, it is a learning aid for reading Scripture. Like a pair of spectacles, it brings the text of Scripture into focus, allowing us to notice things which might otherwise be missed. Doctrine is always under Scripture, its servant rather than its master. Let's explore some of the ways in which theology works.

First, theology sets out to *summarise* what we find in

the Bible. Imagine that someone asks you to tell them what you believe about God. There is so much that you would want to say to them! One of the tasks of theology is to help us summarise the immense richness of the biblical witness to God, Jesus and ourselves. In fact, as we shall see in a later chapter, the doctrine of the Trinity can be seen as a summary of the biblical witness to the person and actions of God.

Suppose you were asked to explain what Christians believe about Jesus Christ. You would find that this takes you some time! You might want to take a series of key scriptural verses, each making an important affirmation about the importance of Jesus. Yet you would not be able to summarise the entire biblical witness to Jesus Christ in a single proof text.

After a while, you might find yourself wondering if there is an easier way of doing this. Is there any way in which the rich (and very extensive) scriptural witness to the identity and importance of Jesus Christ could be summarised in a sentence or two? The theological statement 'Jesus is God and man' aims to do this. It provides a neat outline of the key features of the Christian understanding of the identity and significance of Jesus Christ. Yet it is a *summary* of the biblical teaching, and not a substitute for it.

Second, theology aims to *relate* the ideas we find in the Bible. It brings together biblical statements, and sets out to establish the overall picture to which they point. Individual biblical statements are seen as the bricks which build up the overall picture. They are like brush-strokes, which combine to produce a magnificent picture.

Or they can be thought of as pieces of a jigsaw puzzle. As the pieces are set in place, a pattern is disclosed. Theology aims to put the biblical pieces together, so that we can see the big picture.

At this point, we might want to start going further. We might want to use logic or philosophy to help clarify or develop our thinking. Let's look at a logical argument to see how this works. Suppose that we have two ideas, which we shall call 'A' and 'B'.

1 The Bible teaches A.
2 But if A is true, then so is B.
3 Therefore the Bible also teaches B.

It is not difficult to see how theology can begin from some very simple biblical statements, and then develop these in quite complex directions. Let's look at a classic argument about the identity of Jesus which shows up very clearly how we can build on biblical foundations, and develop more complex ideas.

Christians declare that Jesus is their Saviour. The New Testament frequently refers to Jesus as 'Saviour', and to Christians as those who are being saved. Yet the Old Testament is quite clear that only God can save. So what are the implications of this? Let's set out the ideas, and see how they are related.

1 The Bible teaches that Jesus saves.
2 The Bible teaches that only God can save.

So what is to be concluded from these two statements?

The obvious answer is the following:

3 Therefore the Bible also teaches that Jesus is God.

As we shall see in the following chapter, this is a highly important point. Yet at this stage, our concern is to note how some basic biblical ideas can become the foundation of serious theological reflection.

Theology is thus a voyage of discovery to the heart of the Bible. We could say that theology is about unpacking the implications of biblical statements. It involves taking the trouble to explore and unfold the rich network of ideas that are linked together in the biblical material. One truth is found to lead on to another, and reinforce it.

We will explore this in more detail in the next chapter, by looking at how Christians go about talking about the identity of Jesus Christ.

7

Who is Jesus? Putting the jigsaw together

The greatest jigsaw puzzle the world has ever known is the identity of Jesus. 'Who do you say that I am?' (Mark 8:27–9). To answer this question, we have to put together the many pieces of the New Testament witness to the identity and significance of Jesus. Here are some of them.

First, the New Testament sees Jesus as the fulfilment of the people of Israel. As Matthew's gospel points out so often, Jesus is the fulfilment of Old Testament prophecy. He is the Messiah, the long-awaited deliverer of God's people.

Second, it uses a series of titles to refer to him, each of which tells us something special about him. He is 'Lord' – the same title used to refer to God in the Old Testament. He is the 'Son of God' and the 'Son of Man'. Occasionally, he is even referred to explicitly as 'God'.

Let's look at one of these in detail. The New Testament leaves us in no doubt that Jesus is our Saviour. Jesus is the 'Saviour, who is Christ the Lord' (Luke 2:11). Yet only God can save! This theme is echoed throughout the Old Testament. Israel is regularly reminded that she cannot save herself, nor can she be saved by the idols of the nations round about her. It is the Lord, and the Lord alone, who will save (Isaiah 45:21–2).

In the full knowledge that it was God alone who could save, the first Christians had no hesitation in affirming that *Jesus* was our Saviour. This was no misunderstanding on the part of people who were ignorant of the Old Testament! It was simply a recognition of what Jesus achieved through his cross and resurrection. But who was Jesus, if he did something that only God can do? We can see here a clue to his true identity!

Third, Jesus was raised from the dead by God. This event radiates throughout the New Testament. It is seen as good news for believers, who will share that resurrection. Yet it also tells us something about the identity of Jesus. For Paul, Jesus' resurrection tells us that he is the Son of God (Romans 1:3–4). For Peter, it declares that he is the 'Lord and Messiah' (Acts 2:36).

Fourth, the gospels report things that Jesus said and did which cast light on his identity. An excellent example is provided by Mark's account of how Jesus healed a paralytic (Mark 2:1–12). Jesus tells the paralytic that his sins are forgiven. This provokes outrage and astonishment on the part of the Jewish teachers of the law, who were watching him closely. 'He's blaspheming! Who can forgive sins but God alone?' (Mark 2:7). Those teachers were right. Only God can forgive sin. So what does this tell us about the identity of Jesus?

The simple fact is that Jesus had no right or authority whatsoever to speak those words *if he was just a man*. Yet

Jesus declares that he does have such authority to forgive, and proceeds to heal the man (Mark 2:10–11). Notice how Jesus thus does something which, strictly speaking, only God can do. We see here a very important piece of the jigsaw puzzle. If Jesus does things which only God can do, we have a vitally important clue to his identity.

Many of us enjoy reading crime fiction. Identifying the murderer lies at the heart of just about every good murder mystery. The reader is helped to do this through *clues* – pieces of evidence which build up to help us work out what really happened, and who the murderer really was.

The gospels are also concerned with a mystery – the identity of Jesus. The gospel writers want us to put together all the clues provided by the things Jesus said and did, and work out who he really was. There are many pieces of evidence that must be brought together for the final verdict on the identity of Jesus. Theology aims to put those pieces together, and make sense of them.

So what is the result? What do we get when we put all the pieces together? Two major conclusions result.

First, that Jesus was a genuine human being. He was someone who felt pain, who wept, and who knew what it was like to be hungry and thirsty. Yet this insight, on its own, is not enough to do justice to the biblical portrait of Jesus. We must turn to the second conclusion to understand why.

In the second place, the New Testament insists that Jesus was far more than a human being. Without in any way denying the real humanity of Jesus, the New

Testament declares him to be the Son of God. It applies words to him which are reserved for God, and attributes actions to him which are the privilege of God alone. Jesus is not simply someone who does what only God can do – such as save us, and forgive sins. He is able to do these things because of who he is. Because Jesus is God, he is able to do what God does.

Theology establishes that these two conclusions are, in the first place, necessary, and, in the second place, justified. They are the result of a long and passionate analysis of the total person of Jesus – what he said and did, what was done to him, and how people reacted to him. No other way of thinking about him is capable of doing justice to the biblical evidence.

Theologians refer to these conclusions as 'the two natures of Christ'. They are stated in the Nicene Creed, which refers to Jesus as 'true God and true man'. This may seem like logical weakness – yet it is the only way of doing justice to the full significance of Jesus. Human reason is simply unable to cope with this insight. Yet it is essential to a proper understanding of the identity and importance of Jesus.

To make this point clearer, let us explore the following question. What would happen if we were to give up one of the two insights noted above? For example, it would be a lot simpler if we treated Jesus as a human being, and stopped talking about him as God. That would solve our logical problem at a stroke!

It certainly would. But it would cause fatal problems elsewhere. If Jesus was just a human being, he could not redeem us. Only God can save! He could not reveal God to us. Only God can reveal himself! We would end up with a logically neat understanding of Jesus which distorts his identity and destroys the gospel.

Or we might feel that we could abandon any talk about Jesus being a human. Again, this is logically neat. But it means abandoning too many fundamental gospel insights. If Jesus is not a human being (like us!), then he did not really suffer. He cannot identify with us. Nor can we speak of God entering into our situation to redeem us.

Dorothy L. Sayers stated the situation memorably: 'If Christ was only man, then he is entirely irrelevant to any thought about God; if he is only God, then he is entirely irrelevant to any experience of human life.' Theology shows us why we need to affirm the 'two natures of Christ', and what we lose if we deny it. But above all, it confirms the coherence of the Christian understanding of the identity of Jesus.

A similar situation arises with the doctrine of the Trinity, to which we now turn.

8

The Trinity: the big picture about God

There is a well-known story told about Augustine of Hippo, one of the greatest Christian theologians. Augustine was in the process of writing a very learned book about the Trinity. He took a break to walk along the Mediterranean shoreline. As he wandered along the shore, he noticed a young boy nearby. The boy filled a pail full of seawater, walked a short distance to a hole in the sand, and emptied the water into the hole. He then returned to the sea, and repeated the whole process.

Augustine watched this for some time, then asked the boy what he thought he was doing. 'I am emptying the Mediterranean Sea into this hole in the sand,' he replied. Augustine laughed. 'You will never fit that ocean into that tiny hole! You're wasting your time.' The boy came straight back at him. 'And you are wasting your time writing a book about God. You will never fit God into a book!'

Now some scholars suspect (with good reason!) that this story may well be an invention. But it still makes an

excellent point. We can never do justice to the full wonder of God. The important thing is to make sure that we do everything we can to talk about God as faithfully and fully as we can.

It is this principle which underlies one of the most difficult areas of Christian theology – the doctrine of the Trinity. For many Christians, the idea that there is 'one God in three persons' is difficult to grasp, and seems to make a simple gospel needlessly complicated. But this is not the case. The Christian experience of God is immensely rich. It is vitally important to do justice to this, even if the result seems difficult to understand.

So what are the key elements of the Christian understanding of God? The basic biblical themes which we must insist on including are:

1 Our God is the one who created the world, and all that is in it.
2 Our God redeemed us in Christ on the cross at Calvary.
3 Our God is present with us now in his Spirit.

It might make things much simpler if we reduced our vision of God to just one of these elements. For example, we might suggest that it is good enough to believe in God as our creator. Adding in extra ideas just makes things difficult. But this would be to deny that God redeems us, or that he cares for us. It might be much easier to believe – yet it is an impoverished view of God.

It is essential to do justice to the way God has revealed himself, rather than reducing God so that we can understand him. The doctrine of the Trinity summarises the greatness of God, partly by reminding us of all that God has done. It encourages us to broaden our vision of God. Above all, it demands that we do not falsely limit God by insisting that he fits into our limited understanding!

'What,' asked the *Shorter Westminster Catechism*, 'is the chief end of man?' The answer given is rightly celebrated as a jewel in the Christian theological crown: 'To glorify God and enjoy him for ever'. This brief statement sets us on a journey of theological exploration. It challenges us to gain a fresh apprehension of the glory of God, so that we may return that glory to God and have our spiritual lives enriched by the knowledge of such a God. To catch such a glimpse of the full splendour of God is also a powerful stimulus to evangelism. Was it not by catching a glimpse of the glory of God in the temple that Isaiah responded to the divine call to go forth in service (Isaiah 6:1–9)?

St Patrick, the patron saint of my native Ireland, sets out a vision of God in the great hymn generally known as 'St Patrick's Breastplate'. In this hymn, the believer is constantly reminded of the richness and the depth of the Christian understanding of God, and that this God has been bonded to the believer through faith.

> I bind unto myself today
> The strong name of the Trinity,
> By invocation of the same,
> The Three in One, and One in Three.

The hymn then moves on to survey the vast panorama of the works of God in creation. We are reminded that this God who we have made our own through faith is the same God who brought the earth into being. As we contemplate the wonders of nature, we gain the astonishing insight that the God whose presence and power undergird the world of nature is the same God whose presence and power is channelled into our individual existences:

> I bind unto myself today
> The virtues of the star-lit heaven,
> The glorious sun's life-giving ray,
> The whiteness of the moon at even,
> The flashing of the lightning free,
> The whirling wind's tempestuous shocks,
> The stable earth, the deep salt sea,
> Around the old eternal rocks.

Our attention then turns to the work of God in redemption. The same God who created the world – the earth, the sea, the sun, moon, and stars – acted in Jesus Christ to redeem us. In the history of Jesus Christ, from his incarnation to his second coming, we may see God acting to redeem us, an action which we appropriate and make our own through faith.

> I bind this day to me for ever,
> By power of faith, Christ's incarnation;
> His baptism in Jordan river;
> His death on Cross for my salvation;
> His bursting from the spicèd tomb;
> His riding up the heavenly way;

> His coming at the day of doom;
> I bind unto myself today.

We are invited to reflect upon the history of Jesus Christ: his incarnation, baptism, death, resurrection, ascension and final coming on the last day. And all these, Patrick affirms, are the action of the same God who created us, as he moves to redeem us through Jesus Christ. All these were done for us, for the sinful creatures upon whom a gracious God took pity.

Finally, the God who called the universe into being and redeemed us through the great sequence of events which is the history of Jesus Christ is also the God who is with us here and now, who meets us and stays with us.

> I bind unto myself today
> The power of God to hold and lead,
> His eye to watch, his might to stay,
> His ear to hearken to my need.
> The wisdom of my God to teach,
> His hand to guide, his shield to ward;
> The word of God to give me speech,
> His heavenly host to be my guard.

This is the God that Scripture speaks of, and who we must encounter in our experience – the God who broke the mould of human thinking, forcing us to stretch our ideas and categories to their limits in order to even begin to accommodate his wonder and splendour.

The great medieval theologian Thomas Aquinas once

wrote that theology is not so much about understanding things, as about being forced to our knees in adoration and praise. The doctrine of the Trinity brings home to us the immensity of God's being. It reminds us of all that God has done for us. And in the end, the proper response to this can only be to turn to him in praise and wonder – and to long to bring a knowledge of this wonderful God to those who have yet to discover him.

In this chapter, we touched on the theme of the doctrine of creation. The following chapter will deal with this doctrine in more detail, because it allows us to look at another aspect of Christian theology. Theology helps us to make connections between the different aspects of our faith. It lays foundations on which we can build, forging links between faith and life. In what follows, we shall explore this theme of 'making connections' by looking at the doctrine of creation in greater detail.

9

Making connections: the doctrine of creation

The Christian faith declares that God is the creator of this world. How are we to make sense of this? And what difference does it make to the way in which we think and live?

The doctrine of creation brings together the insights of many biblical passages. Perhaps most obviously, it builds on the great themes of Genesis 1–2, which stress that God created every aspect of the world, including ourselves. Yet other biblical themes are also important, including the idea that God imposes order upon chaos (see, for example, Isaiah 29:16; 44:8; Jeremiah 18:1–6).

The Genesis creation account reminds us that everything in this world is the work of God. Many in the Ancient Near East believed that the sun and moon were gods, and were fearful of them. They had to be worshipped in the right way; if they were not, they might withhold their light and plunge the world into darkness. Christians do not need to fear the sun or moon. They were created by God (Genesis 1:14–18), and are under his authority.

We also learn that men and women have been created in the image of God (Genesis 1:26–7). This distinguished human beings from all other created beings. Being created 'in the image of God' includes the ability to relate to God. In other words, God creates us with the intention of establishing a personal relationship between himself and us. To have the 'image of God' implies some kind of likeness between ourselves and God – but not an identity. We are not divine; rather, we are created for the purpose of relating to God. Sin frustrates that purpose, which is only realised through the redemption brought by Christ. Christ's saving death allows us to enter into this cherished and transforming relationship with God.

Two analogies are helpful as we attempt to make sense of this important doctrine. The first is to think of God as a builder or a master craftsman. We can think of God as both an architect and a builder – someone who both designed and constructed a beautiful building. The wisdom of God can thus be seen in the marvellous way in which the world is put together.

St Paul's Cathedral, London, is one of the greatest works of the architect Sir Christopher Wren. There is no memorial to Wren in that cathedral – just an inscription over its north door: 'If you are looking for a memorial, look around you.' The genius and wisdom of the architect can be seen in what he built. So we can see God's wisdom in the creation. 'The heavens declare the glory of God!' (Psalm 19:1).

The second helpful analogy is that of an artist – perhaps a famous painter or sculptor. Something of the artist's personality and genius can be seen in the work of art itself. In the same way, the wisdom and love of God can be seen in the beauty of creation. It is thus no wonder that so many natural scientists are active Christian believers. To study creation in such detail is to come into close contact with the works of God himself.

But what difference does this make to the way we think and act? There must be a connection between theology and lifestyle – between what we believe and the way we behave. James asks us to be doers and not merely hearers of the word (James 1:22). So what difference does the doctrine of creation make?

The first point that the doctrine of creation makes is that the world belongs to God. It is not ours. We did not make it. Adam was placed in the Garden of Eden to take care of it (Genesis 2:15). This is a vitally important insight. We are the *stewards*, not the *owners*, of God's creation. God has entrusted his good creation to us, and will hold us accountable for the use which we make of it.

This insight underlies a proper Christian concern for the environment. We are called to be earth-keepers, people who tend what God has made and entrusted to us. We simply do not have the right to exploit the world for our own profit. It is God's, not ours. As Adam was called to tend Eden, so we are called to share in this creation mandate. This insight must change the way we behave towards creation, and encourage us to respect and care for it as God's treasured possession.

We could set this out in terms of four propositions:

1 The natural order, including human beings, is the

result of God's act of creation, and is affirmed to be God's possession.

2 Human beings are distinguished from the remainder of creation because we are created in the 'image of God'.

3 We are charged with the tending of creation (as Adam was entrusted with the care of Eden), knowing that this creation is the cherished possession of God.

4 So there is no theological reason for asserting that humanity has the 'right' to do what it pleases with the natural order. The creation is God's, and he has entrusted it to us. We are to care for it, not exploit it.

The doctrine of creation also allows us another significant insight. *The creation is God's, not God.* Some religions, including some forms of paganism which have enjoyed a fashionable revival in recent years, argue that nature is divine. Christians adopt a significantly different approach. Nature is created by God. It is not divine, but something of God's nature and character can be known through it.

We need to draw a line between the creator and the creation. Everything on our side of the line – including ourselves! – is God's creation, not something which is in itself divine. There is no place in Christianity for the worship of nature (a point made in detail by Paul in Romans 1–2). God alone is to be worshipped. Yet we must respect and care for nature as the work of the same God who loves and redeemed us. To love God is to love the works of God – including the creation.

Finally, we note that the doctrine of creation is also

important for Christian apologetics – that is, the defence of the Christian faith to outsiders. It is often difficult for someone who is not a Christian to conceive of God. The idea of 'God' may seem empty, abstract and formless to such a person. The doctrine of creation reminds us that God may be known, if only to a limited extent, through the created world. God provides visible and tangible pointers to his invisible and intangible reality.

Creation is like a signpost, pointing away from itself to its creator – but holding our attention, because it is something we can see and feel. To progress no further than the signpost, worshipping it rather than its goal, is to lapse into nature religion. But to follow the direction in which the sign points is to arrive at a true knowledge of the living God, intimated in creation and given its full and glorious substance in Scripture and in Jesus Christ.

One of the finest statements of the appeal to the creation can be seen in the writings of Jonathan Edwards (1703–58), probably the greatest theologian to emerge from the United States of America. Edwards declares that 'the Son of God created the world . . . to communicate himself in an image of his own excellency . . . He communicates a sort of shadow . . . of his excellencies . . . so that when we are delighted with flowery meadows and gentle breezes . . . we may consider that we see only the emanation of the sweet benevolence of Jesus Christ.'[2] Thus a sense of the beauty of creation, caught while

[2] *Cited by Robert W. Jenson,* America's Theologian: A Recommendation of Jonathan Edwards *(New York: Oxford University Press, 1988), p. 19.*

walking along the side of a river, points to the beauty of God himself as its creator.

This naturally leads us to think about further ways in which theology can help us explain and communicate the Christian faith to our friends. In the following chapter, we will look at how theology allows us to develop powerful approaches to apologetics. Good theology is an essential tool for evangelism!

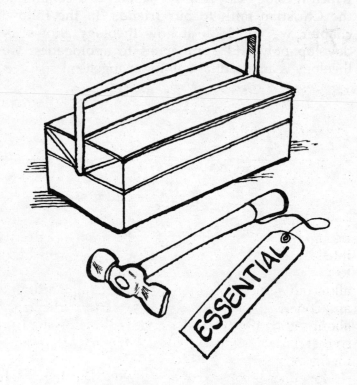

10

The attractiveness of the gospel: theology and apologetics

Apologetics is about giving reasons for faith. It is about persuading people that Christianity makes sense. Becoming a Christian does not mean committing intellectual suicide. Apologetics aims to deal with barriers to faith, giving reasoned and thoughtful replies which allow our audience to appreciate to the full the attraction and coherence of the Christian faith. In particular, it is about setting out the full attractiveness of Jesus Christ, so that those outside the faith can begin to grasp why he merits very serious consideration.

How does theology come into this? Theology enables us to appreciate our faith for all its worth. That is good news for us: it deepens the quality of our faith. But it also allows us to begin to appreciate why Christianity might be attractive to others.

Jesus once compared the kingdom of heaven to a pearl

of great price. 'The kingdom of heaven is like a merchant looking for fine pearls. When he found one of great value, he went away and sold everything he had and bought it' (Matthew 13:45–6). The merchant knew about pearls, and he could see that this was so beautiful and valuable that it was worth giving up everything so that he could possess it.

Our task is to help people realise that the Christian faith is so exciting and wonderful that nothing else can be compared to it. This means helping people to grasp the attractiveness of the faith. Theology allows us to identify and appreciate the individual elements of the Christian faith. It is like someone opening a treasure chest, and holding up jewels, pearls and precious metals, one by one, so that each may be seen individually and appreciated.

It may be helpful to offer an illustration of the relation of apologetics, theology and evangelism. Jesus often compared the gospel to a feast, or some kind of great party (for example, see Luke 14:15–24). Try to imagine three different ways of getting people to come to that party.

The first approach stresses that there really is a party, explains why it is going to be great fun, and reflects on the great time that everyone is going to have. This is what *apologetics* is all about. Apologetics is basically about affirming the truth and the attraction of the gospel. It is a kind of pre-evangelism. It prepares the way for an invitation to be issued, by helping people to understand what Christianity is about, and why it is so attractive and meaningful.

The second approach focusses on the individual dishes which will be served. It identifies each of these dishes, and allows its attractions to be savoured. The wonderful vintage wines; the fresh and fragrant bread; the succulent fruit. All are named and relished. This is what *theology* does. It invites us to wander around the heavily laden table, and marvel at the riches set out before us. It makes it easier for us to invite people to that feast, because we can tell them exactly what awaits them.

Third, *evangelism* is about issuing a personal invitation to come to faith and become a Christian. Yet theology has laid the ground for issuing that invitation. Just as a prism breaks a beam of white light into the beautiful colours of the rainbow, so theology allows us to separate out the individual elements of the Christian gospel. Theology is the tool which allows the many facets of the gospel to scintillate brilliantly in its light.

But why is this important? Why should anyone want to explore the many facets of the gospel? The answer lies in the audiences to which we present the gospel. Different people have different needs and concerns. One aspect of the gospel may interlock with one group of needs, while another may match up with others. To appreciate this point, let us return to look briefly once more at a central theme of the Christian faith – the meaning of the cross.

It is impossible to summarise the immensely rich and complex message of the cross in a few words. Indeed, one of the great delights of theology is that it offers us the opportunity of reflecting deeply (and at leisure!) on the full meaning of the great themes of the Christian message, such as the cross of Christ. Yet it is important to note that a number of aspects can be identified within that message – each of which has particular relevance to certain groups of people.

One great theme of the gospel is that the cross and resurrection of Jesus Christ free us from the fear of death. Christ has been raised from the dead, and those who have faith will one day share in that resurrection, and be with him for ever. Death is no longer something that need be feared. We celebrate this supremely at Easter. This great message of hope in the face of suffering and death is crucial for us all. Yet it has a special relevance to those many people who wake up in the middle of the night, frightened by the thought of death.

Another great theme of the cross is that of forgiveness. Through the death of Christ, real forgiveness of our sins is possible. This helps us to understand that our redemption is both precious and costly. Yet it also helps us appreciate the relevance of the gospel to a particular group of people – those who are burdened by guilt. Many feel that they can hardly continue living on account of that guilt. Theology identifies one of the many facets of the gospel which has especial relevance to those people. Those sins can be forgiven, and their guilt washed away.

The same type of thinking can be applied again and again. The important thing is to bring the gospel into contact with people's lives. Theology helps us identify the most appropriate point of contact with individuals, so that they can discover the joy of faith. This doesn't mean that we are reducing the gospel to just one point! It simply means that we are looking for the aspect of the gospel which is of greatest relevance to the person we are talking to. The rest of the gospel will follow in due course. We have to start somewhere – and theology helps identify the best starting point in each case.

Theology, then, helps us explain and proclaim the Christian faith more effectively to people who are not yet Christians. It is an essential tool for individuals and churches as they aim to proclaim the gospel for all its worth. But theology has another role, related to this. It does not merely help us to understand the attractiveness of the gospel to others. It deepens our own understanding of the gospel, and helps us apply it to ourselves.

We have just looked at the relevance of theology to apologetics. Now we will consider its relevance to spirituality.

11

Sounding the depths of faith: theology and spirituality

Spirituality is about the application of Christian truth to the life of faith. It aims to ensure that we both *know about* God and *know* God. It seeks to apply God to our hearts as well as our minds. Spirituality deals with the deepening of our personal knowledge of God. But, as we shall see, spirituality is grounded in good theology. Theology thus provides us with a secure foundation for Christian living.

One of the most important theologians to write in this field in the twentieth century is James I. Packer (born 1926). Packer's classic work *Knowing God* is an excellent example of a book which shows how good theology leads to a deepening of faith and the enrichment of personal experience. Although Packer values the importance of careful thinking about the faith, he is clear that Christianity is about more than ideas! It is about allowing the reality of God to penetrate every aspect of our life.

On 11 December 1989, Packer delivered his inaugural lecture at Regent College, Vancouver, on the relation of

theology and spirituality. In that lecture, Packer stressed the utter impossibility of separating theology and spirituality:[3]

> I question the adequacy of conceptualizing the subject-matter of systematic theology as simply revealed truths about God, and I challenge the assumption that has usually accompanied this form of statement, that the material, like other scientific data, is best studied in cool and clinical detachment. Detachment from what, you ask? Why, from the relational activity of trusting, loving, worshipping, obeying, serving and glorifying God: the activity that results from realizing that one is actually in God's presence, actually being addressed by him, every time one opens the Bible or reflects on any divine truth whatsoever. This ... proceeds as if doctrinal study would only be muddled by introducing devotional concerns; it drives a wedge between ... knowing true notions about God and knowing the true God himself.

Packer's point is that a genuine experience of God makes the detached study of God impossible. To know God is to be committed to him. To drive a wedge between theology and spirituality is like asking two people who are in love to behave coldly towards each other.

So how does theology help us spiritually? How does it help us sustain and deepen our faith? To answer this question, we shall explore an aspect of theology that we

[3] James I. Packer, 'An Introduction to Systematic Spirituality', Crux 26 No. 1 (March 1990), pp. 2–8; quote at p. 6.

have not yet looked at in this little volume – the problem of suffering and pain.

How can we cope with suffering? This is one of the most distressing aspects of life. One of the reasons why it is so distressing is that it is something that we often feel lies beyond God. How can we pray to God about our suffering, when he does not know for himself what it is like? It would be so much easier if God had experienced suffering and pain at first hand.

It is always easier to relate to someone who has been through the same experience as us. Suppose that a close friend of mine had died, and I wanted to talk to someone who would be a good listener. I could go to someone who had not had this experience, but was prepared to try and understand what I was going through. That might be helpful, and it would certainly be better than nothing.

Yet it would be far more useful to me to talk to someone who had been through the same experience. There would be a bond of sympathy between us. We would have shared a common sorrow, and be able to understand each other. I would be much more positive about speaking to someone who had already been through what I was now experiencing. It is therefore entirely understandable that we would find it much easier to pray to God about suffering and pain if we knew that he had been there before us.

So does God suffer? This is one of the most poignant questions confronting many Christians, particularly those who are going through a period of suffering themselves. It makes all the difference in the world whether God has experienced suffering at first hand. If

God does not know what suffering is, then God will not be able to sympathise with us in our sufferings. On the other hand, if God has experienced the suffering and pain of this world, we can turn to God in prayer knowing that we are in the presence of a fellow-sufferer who knows what we are going through and can understand our experience, fears and concerns.

It is here that theology comes into the scene, and it has a decisive contribution to make. It reminds us that Jesus is none other than the Son of God. In Jesus Christ, God has entered into our world of sorrow and pain in order to redeem us. The argument for God's first-hand experience of suffering is based upon the 'two natures' of Jesus, which we considered earlier. The argument may be set out as follows:

1 Jesus is God.
2 Jesus experienced pain and suffering.
3 Therefore God experienced pain and suffering.

With this thought in mind, we can turn again to suffering and pain. These are like strange lands, in which God chose to live before us. He has already experienced the suffering and pain which we now know. God has dignified suffering by passing through it himself.

That thought does not take suffering away. Yet it does allow us to see it in a new light. God suffered in Christ. God knows what it is like to suffer. The letter to the Hebrews talks about Jesus being our 'sympathetic High Priest' (Hebrews 4:15) – someone who suffers along with us (which is the literal meaning of both the Greek word

sympathetic and the Latin word *compassionate*). God knows how weak our faith is, and does all he can to sustain and support it from his side. The suffering of Jesus Christ is meant to reassure us that we have the privilege of relating to a God who knows the pain and sorrow of living in a fallen world. The passion stories of the gospels tell of a Saviour who really understands suffering, and who has been through it himself.

The God who made heaven and earth knows what it is like to be human. This is at one and the same time an astonishing and deeply comforting thought. We are not talking about God becoming like us, just as if he was putting on some sort of disguise so that he could be passed off as one of us. We are talking about the God who created the world entering into that same world as one of us and on our behalf, in order to redeem us. God has not sent a messenger or a representative to help the poor creatures that we are; he has involved himself directly, redeeming his own creation, instead of getting someone else to do it for him.

Getting our ideas about God right is essential to our Christian living. If we think that God has never got involved in the pain and sadness of the world, we will find it difficult to relate to him, and even more difficult to pray when we suffer.

The God who Christians adore and worship is one who humbled himself, entered into our sad and sorrowful world, and bore those sorrows so that we might be redeemed, and have the hope of eternal life. One day we shall be with him in the New Jerusalem, when all pain and sorrow will finally be taken away.

12

Moving on

Every book has its limits, and this one is no exception.
Its goals have been limited. We could summarise them
like this:

1 To introduce you to the study of theology.
2 To show you that it is worthwhile.
3 To encourage you to take it further.

There is far more that needs to be said about theology!
Limits on space mean that important subjects have only
been touched on, and major themes treated very super-
ficially. You will often have found yourself wishing that
it was possible to explore things in greater depth.

So why not do this? Why not take things further for
yourself? This book has tried to encourage you in this,
by showing you that you can handle some basic theological principles. There is gold in those theological hills!
Why not explore things further?

Good theology can bring a new depth and quality to
your faith. It will deepen your understanding, and help
you explain your faith more effectively to your friends.

You began as an amateur. But you don't need to stay one. You could be a very important resource person for your church, or your Bible study group. You could find yourself giving much better answers to those questions about Christianity that people ask you at work.

If you feel ready to move on, this final chapter will help you to work out how best to proceed.

There are two main ways in which you can take your interest in theology further. Broadly speaking, they are to move on to the more detailed study of theology as a whole, or to begin to study one or two theologians in greater depth.

This volume has not been able to examine any area of theology in any depth. I have had to omit discussion of huge areas of interest due to lack of space. A more detailed introduction to Christian theology will allow much fuller discussion. For example, you could expect to find discussion of the following important matters:

1 The sources of theology. How does theology make use of and relate to the Bible, reason, tradition and experience?
2 Major periods of theology. For example, the sixteenth century is one of the most interesting periods in Christian theology. It allows you to learn about theologians such as Martin Luther (1483–1546) and John Calvin (1509–64), or great theological issues such as justification by faith.

Two of the most widely used introductions to Christian theology may be noted here.

Millard J. Erickson's *Christian Theology* is a very substantial work, which offers a thorough and even-handed assessment of many areas of theology.[4] Erickson has a long history of involvement in theological education, and this work is clearly written by an experienced teacher and guide.

The second introduction is basically a big brother to this little work. My *Christian Theology: An Introduction* offers an entry-level introduction to the leading questions of Christian theology.[5] It is written on the basis of the assumption that you know nothing about theology or Christian history, and sets itself the target of getting you up to speed as quickly as possible. A set of annotated readings is also available, to encourage you to read the original works of theologians.[6]

This brings us to the second way of developing your growing interest in theology – reading the works of some leading theologians. Clearly, this raises a major question: which theologians should I read?

As this book is written at an introductory level, the best answer is perhaps the simplest. *Read the theologians who write well.* There is no point in trying to read a major theologian if this is going to be a very difficult experience. Wait until you feel confident enough to do this! In the meantime, begin to explore some theologians who are

[4] Millard J. Erickson, Christian Theology, *second edition (Grand Rapids: Baker Book House, 1998).*

[5] *Alister E. McGrath,* Christian Theology: An Introduction, *second edition (Oxford: Blackwell Publishing, 1997).*

[6] *Alister E. McGrath,* The Christian Theology Reader *(Oxford: Blackwell Publishing, 1995).*

noted for their clear and accessible writing style.

Begin by reading a biography of the theologian. This will help you to realise that the theologian in question is a real person! It will also help you get an idea of the issues they wrestled with, the answers they gave, and their importance for the Christian faith.

Now there are many theologians who fall into this category. Augustine of Hippo, Martin Luther and John Calvin are obvious examples. However, the two I will recommend are both twentieth-century writers who have had considerable influence over English-language Christianity, especially at a popular level.

C. S. Lewis (1888–1963) is remembered for his *Chronicles of Narnia*, a series of finely written stories for children which set out basic Christian ideas in an extremely imaginative and attractive form.[7] His more serious theological works – such as *Surprised by Joy* and *Mere Christianity* – offer a very well-argued and highly readable account of the basic themes of the Christian faith.[8] Lewis was noted as a very skilful communicator, and exploring his writings is an enjoyable and effective way of furthering your interest in theology.

James I. Packer (1926–) is one of the most highly regarded evangelical theologians of the twentieth century. He studied theology at Oxford University, and

[7]*C. S. Lewis,* Chronicles of Narnia, *volumes 1–7, Paperback Edition (London: Collins, 1980).*
[8]*C. S. Lewis,* Surprised by Joy, *Centenary Edition (London: Fount, 1998).*
C. S. Lewis, Mere Christianity, *Centenary Edition (London: Fount, 1997).*

gained a doctorate for his thesis on the theology of a leading Puritan writer. Packer soon established himself as a highly effective theological teacher, with a particular interest in relating Christian theology and spirituality. This is most evident in his best-known work, *Knowing God*.[9] Packer had a particular interest in the theology of the Puritans; his *Quest for Godliness* (published in the United Kingdom as *Among God's Giants*) explored the Puritan vision of the Christian life, and its relevance for today.[10]

Conclusion

Studying theology is like throwing open a door. Inside lies a myriad of treasures. We are allowed to pick these up, one at a time, and marvel at their beauty and richness. To throw open the door on the treasure-house of Christian theology is to examine each of the great themes of the faith.

Each of these themes, like a precious jewel, deserves careful and individual attention. Each has so much to offer. Each can dazzle our minds, excite our hearts, and make us long to preach the good news.

For theology is not about cold and clinical detachment, nor dry and dull formulas and phrases. It is about learning more about the loving and living God, and

[9] J. I. *Packer*, Knowing God, *Second Edition with Study Guide (London: Hodder & Stoughton, 1993)*.
[10] J. I. *Packer*, Among God's Giants *(Eastbourne: Kingsway, 1991)*.

serving him with all our minds as well as our hearts. To learn more about God is to draw closer to him, and to look forward with anticipation to the day when we shall finally be with him.

In the meantime, there is much to be done. The gospel must be preached. Faith must be strengthened. God must be served. And in all these tasks, theology can both inspire and inform us. Theology is 'talk about God' which deepens our longing finally to be with God, and nourishes our longing to serve him in the meanwhile.

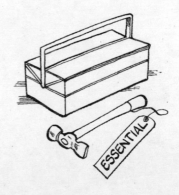

Also in this series

Evangelism For Amateurs

Michael Green

EVANGELISM MAKES MOST OF US FEEL TOTALLY INADEQUATE

We simply feel like running for cover: the last thing we want to be seen as is mindless enthusiasts pushing our views on other people. But if we are to follow Jesus' command to go and make disciples, it isn't something we can just ignore.

EVANGELISM FOR AMATEURS is full of ideas on reaching out to our families, friends and neighbours in a way that is relaxed, 'human', and possible even to those of us who feel unqualified for the job.

There are guidelines for talking to those who feel that 'my view is as good as yours', or for whom churchgoing is something they wouldn't normally even consider, making this book highly relevant to today's cultural climate.

Rather than 'highjacking' people with the gospel, we can confidently begin to help them find a living faith for themselves.

Hodder & Stoughton
0 340 71420 4